Jdg
Poems of Love

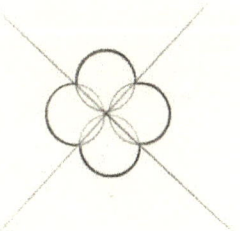

Elizabeth Anne Hin

Copyright © 2016 Elizabeth Anne Hin

All Rights Reserved

Art Copyright © 2016 by Cynthia L. Kirkwood

Editing and Design by Sarla V. J. Matsumura

Library of Congress Control Number: 2016907046

ISBN-13: 978-0692582794
ISBN-10: 0692582797

Printed in the United States of America
Published by Issa Press
Austin, Texas

DEDICATION

To John David Gabriel

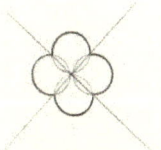

CONTENTS

On Your Birthday	1
God's Will	3
Too Good To Be True	5
As It Should Be	11
Roses	13
On This Valentine's Day	19
Poem for Beth	29
Variations on Jdg's Poem	31
No	35
Sedona	39
Your Hands	47
Rodeo	67
Entrust	69
Your Wife	71
Her Husband	73
White	75
Noble	77
Poem for a Stoic	79
You Were There	83
True Marriage	85
When You Kiss	89
You	91

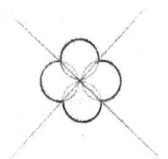

ON YOUR BIRTHDAY

I was awakened
By
Gentle
Flashes
Of light
By
Flickers
Of light
As
I thought
Of you
At early
Morning
In the Desert
On your birthday.

I was awakened
By
Flickers
Of light
In the
Dark
Of the
Predawn sky
So gentle
I was not
Certain
At first

What
They were
And then
It rained
One thunderclap.

It rained
In the Desert
On your birthday
For the Hopi
The greatest blessing
Of all
Beside a sacred path
Love
True marriage
And children
Always.

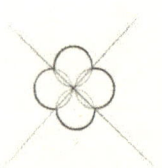

GOD'S WILL

This morning
In my sleep
You came
To me
At the hearth
Of
The Desert
Home
As you showed
A book
To me
Your
Left
Hand
Brushed
My right
So clear
And certain
And courtly
That
I knew
Eternity
Was God's will
For us.

TOO GOOD TO BE TRUE

I.
Every day
I awake
from a thousand
miles away
with beauty in
my heart
for you.
Your history
and your mind
almost
always
say
this
is
too good
to be true.

II.
Other men
seek
this
and
I
do not
give
this
beauty

to
them

It is
not
theirs,

It
is
ours,
beloved.

It
is
true.

III.
I was with
your elder children
in my Desert

We sat
with
their Mother
beneath a lovely
small tree

And there
were Sparrows
too good
to be true.

They sat
all fluffed
in the tree,
as a cool
winter front
moved in
luminous clouds
all morning
during
your
elder children's
honors,
fat
adorable,
being
fed
crumbs,
as we celebrated,
from the
sandwich
of your son
too good
to be true.

IV.
They flew
to
the ground
female and male
near
my
beloved
dog
too good
to be true.

V.
They
are
the French
endearment
I have
given
the beauty
of your
elder daughter's
soul
too good
to be true.

VI.
And the
Mother
of your
children
in hearing
me
speak
of
one of
my two
favorite
birds,
the
Sparrow,
said
the
children's
Father
loves a
small
bird
too,
a songbird
similar
to my
Sparrows
to these
precious
ones.

VII.
I remarked,
a Finch
red,
yellow,
too good
to be true.
Her speaking
of you
with memories
of your nature
to tell your
children
not hateful
but beautiful is
too good
to be true.

VIII.
As you and I
for you
your history
your intelligent mind
too good
to be true
.
Yet,
true.

Marfa, Texas

AS IT SHOULD BE

I
Awoke
This morning
Love
To
Find
That
You
Were gone
To
Heal patients
And
Hear music
And
Call
The
Wildflowers
Of
Texas
To Bloom.

Easter Monday

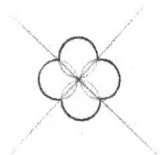

ROSES

There
were
Not
Roses
He did
Not
Wish her
He had
wished
someone else
She had
left
And there
were
not
Roses
Their perfume
had been
For
someone else
And there
were
not
Roses
He did
not
ever
wish

anyone
To
love him
There were
not
romantic gifts
There was
not
to be
romance
He
had
given
promises
In gifts
precious
to him
In sentiments
and
grace
They
had
been
sold
Discarded
And left
by the side
Of the
road

As
garbage
And
there were
not
words
Their
sentiment
was
for others
For Others
He
had wished
There were
not
embraces
His arms
had fallen
off
his shoulders
For
sorrow
Of
discarded sighs
And
caresses
And
promises
Promises

which
were real
For
him
There
were
not
kisses
There
had been
for others
But
no
kisses
No
promises
No
words
Or
His
very breath
Would
Die
Fall
away
forever
If
one more
Word
Kiss

Caress
Embrace
Gift
Rose
Were
discarded
From
the offering
of
His
sweet soul
She
received
All
of these
And
knew
love
For him
He
would
not
love
He did
not
Wish her
As he
offered her
all Roses
Their holy

and real
perfume
Every
romantic gift
Caress
Embrace
Kiss
And
Word

Saint Mary's, Florida

ON THIS VALENTINE'S DAY

In history
in religion
we
say
he was
a saint

Valentine
abiding
in
ancient
Rome
sending
his love
to us
his way
from
across
time

Kind
true
to
everyone
as he
was able.

And so
shall we be

Some
day
some
Valentine's
Day
I shall
tell you
how
in Vietnam
they
follow
him
this
day
like
a Buddha
of
love

Single
Roses
given
to
loves
to
every
kind

of love
Mothers
Fathers
Sweethearts
Spouses
Children

Promenades
rides
through town
on bicycles
scooters
motorcycles
automobiles

Sweet
dinners
and inner
practice
to become
like
Valentine

On his
day

I send
you
my
love

From
a thousand
miles away

From
sleeping
beside
you
at the fire

Upon the
parquet floor
of your
beautiful
sad
home

A home
like
a flower
at bud
in springtime
this
Valentine's
Day

The sadness
to blossom
into
a perfume
of
all life

From
your
Great
Grandmother's
and
Grandmother's
chair
delicate
curved
honey wood
honeyed
rose velvet
rocking
tender
sweet
and feminine

At the
fireplace
talking

Visiting
I believe
you so
beautifully
say
in the South

Absolutely content
in that chair

And you
in
your new
Oak
rocking chair
my beloved
Texan

Sipping coffee

From
your
many mugs

I will
never forget
how
tenderly
you
poured

coffee
and cream
for me
for you

And
so
tenderly
set
the mug
pale beige
hunter green
script
from
the
Waldorf Astoria

At
my place

After spending
the night
in a chair
tending
your Mother
I will never
forget

As our
love
enters
an abiding
place
bringing me
to you
you
to me
to
God

And
because
of this
to everyone
and everything

My
Desert Wren
sings
his
Valentine
to all
this
morning

The very
song
of
blessing
home
and
joy
he sings
every day
outside
my
Desert door

A Valentine
for you
Darling

From
everywhere.

Van Horn, Texas and Cave Creek, Arizona

POEM FOR BETH

I can hear the Wind
Rustling
Hustling
Through the trees and hills
Everywhere
At once
Invisible
Mysterious
Ceaselessly moving
Swirling
Searching
Pushing its way
Over the land
Then silent
A brief pause
Quiet
Is it listening for me?

By Jdg

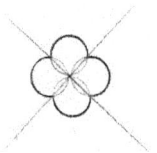

VARIATIONS ON JDG'S POEM

I.

My Darling can hear the wind.
Rustling.
Hustling.
Across his trees, wildflowers and their tender leaves,
On every hill.
He hears it everywhere
Every moment.
He cannot see it.
He knows its mystery.
Ceaselessly moving
Swirling.
Searching.
Pressing its way
Over the land.
Then silent

Like him.

A brief pause, as he breathes, and the wind supports him.
Quiet
Is it listening for him?
Darling, can you not hear its embrace of you,
Your soul,
Your life
Of beauty
And grace?
Listen.

The wind speaks to you again,
Embraces you everywhere
Always.

II.
Is that the wind?
Rustling.
Hustling.
Through your beloved trees and verdant hills.
It sounds everywhere.
It is immediate.
I cannot see it.
In the dear mystery of God.
Ceaselessly moving.
Swirling.
Searching, what is it searching ... it is searching for you,
Darling.
Pushing its way
Over the land
Then silent
A brief pause
Quiet.
It has found you.

III.
In Hinduism Hanuman
Is the Son of the Wind.
The Creator
That Great One
Gave him Hanuman
Several
Great souls to care for
With difficult
Challenging destinies.
One of them
Lord Rama
Challenged Hanuman
Doubting him fearing Hanuman
Had betrayed Lord Rama's Wife.
Hanuman ripped open his chest
And on every cell of
This Son of the Wind
Was written the Name of God.
You can hear the Wind
Is it listening for you?

You
Are made of the Wind
Darling
Hanuman's Brother
You are its second son.

NO!

I
cannot
invite
you to my soul
my lips
the song of my life
or
my bed.

My
husband
is
resting
beneath
its mahogany arch
tired
his
heart
full
yet
empty
from this life.

I
must
say no
to you.

Your
gifts
the Roses
the telephone
calls
pleading
that we
could
dwell
anyplace
someplace
my place
near your
family
mountains
Desert
cities
sun.

This year
alone
there
have been
seven of you.

And
I
have said
no.

I must
say no.

My husband
is
resting.

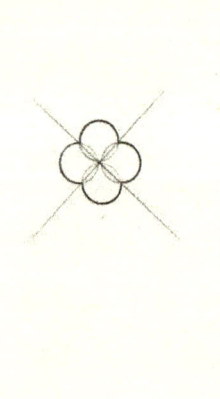

SEDONA

Today
I
do
not know
who is
holding
me
more deeply
God
or
you.

Maybe
it
is
because
you
are
holding
me
from
within
Him.

I
arose
to
watch
the
sun's
rise.

Four men
asked
me
to
marry them
or
to
live
where
I
live
in
this
year
of
death.

As I
breathe
once
again
after

death
and
death
and
death.

Maybe
I
would
teach
and
teaching
in
New Zealand
and
living
at my
younger brother's
if
death
too
strong
still
and
a Doctorate
completed
in another
state
and
teaching

at
a
college
or
community
college
or
university
or
second
grade
or
high
school
because
you
know
I love
children.

I
who never
bore
them
because
you
were
not
there
yet.

Although
eighteen
men
now nineteen
have
asked for
my hand
and heart
and soul.

And
so
very
many
for
every
other
form
of
lover's
union.

No.
He is
not
here
yet.

The
soul
the
man.

The
precious
hand
which
answered
them
all.

These
men.

Your
hand
curled
about
my
other
hand
your
my
own
hand.

Both
of
your
hands
and
both
of
mine.

As I
awakened
with
Cathedral
Rock
in
the dawn.

With the
embrace
of you
from
a
thousand
miles
away.

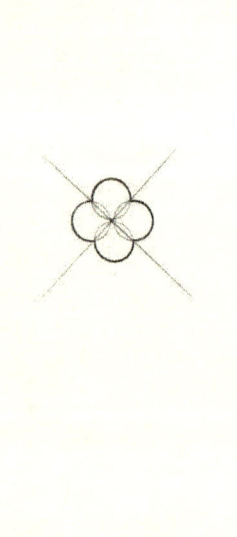

YOUR HANDS

Late
At night
I spoke
To you
Of your hands
By telephone
From

A thousand miles
Away

It was
In
The autumn
I remember
Quietly
I said

I have told
Your son

He has
His Father's hands

Long
Slender
Elegant
Those are

The words
I spoke

And now

Sensitive
Strong
Hands
Which heal
Many
Which seek
Books

Which stroke
A magnificent
Cat
And linger

Upon
A favorite mug

Warmth
Arising through
The cup
From coffee
Treasured
As a moment

Of rest
For your hands

For
Your hands
Every day
Is a
Philosopher's
Stone
Crafted

By soul
Heart
Penetrating
Mind
Splendid
Capacities
Of Understanding

And
True Care

You
The philosopher

Seek
The Logos
Through
Your
Hands

You
Never
Tell Anyone
Not

Anyone
Ever

Not
Even
The animals
You are
Silent
Still
Transparent
True

As God
And you
Move
Together
As one

Through
Your hands

I know
Your hands

Palms
Toward
Heaven
Seeking
Authentic
Refreshment
They
Hold
A glass
Of wine
Holy wine
Earthly wine

You
Express
Not ever
Having
Been

Cherished
Completely

Always
Almost
Enough

Seeking
The Holy Grail
As you
Find
Her Cup
Of wine
Destiny
Eternity
Sacred
Pouring through
Everything
Her spirit
The very

Milky Way
Of your path

Gambling
Too little
Too much
And alcohol
Too little
Never
Not Ever
Too much
Never
Too much
Purchasing
Modest
Objects

Which
The hands
Hope
Assuage
The unfulfilled

Loneliness
Of the

Great
Heart

That
Heart
A
Veritable
Rose
Window

For
The Logos

In every
Language

You stand
Timeless
Suited
A dark silk tie
Shimmering

In the colors
Of
Your aging hair

Turned
Silver

Charcoal
And dark

And
Your
Aging hands
Wise
Kind
And generous
As they
Awaken

Through
The years

Decades
Now

For
You are
Not
Young
Nor

Are your
Lovely hands

Your hands
Which
Are
Cared for
Marked
Strained
By events

Cannot
Be veiled

They reveal
The purity
Of your quest
The dedication

Of now
And of eons

Your hands
Playing
Games
Exploring
Technology

Writing
A prescription

A message
A tip
On a
Café
Charge card

Revering
The past

The future

In
Tremendous
Humor
Remarkable
Insight
And

Penetrating
Love

So profound
It frightens
Even you
But it does not

Frighten
Your hands

Never
Has any
Breath
Even
One breath
Arising
Into
The next

Of God's
Spirit
Frightened
Your hands

Your hands
Play music

In critical
Brilliance
In outrage
In seeking
Sometimes
In happiness
In memory
In play
In wit
In passion
In loss
In fulfillment

And
In nature

Your hands
Throw
A ball
For
Treasured
Dogs
An eternal
Human
Gesture
Of love

I know
That one

Your hands
Remember
Childhood
Not understanding
Why these parents
Why this place
Where is
All
That
I love
Your hands
In school
At work

With family
Driving
Playing
Tennis
Golf
Microwave buttons
Computer and
Piano
Keys
Fine
Silverware
At
Restaurants
Guitar

And violin
Strings
Against fingers
The touch
Of horsehair

Bow
To skin

Keys
Clubs
Hotel keys
Pens
To sign
In

At
Conferences

Soothing
A tendril
Of
Your hair
Back
Away
From
Your face

From
The touch
Of
The wind

And
From
Your brow
Midday
After
Probing
The answers

For
A kind

Or a difficult
Patient

Stroking
Your beard
Pensive
Reflective
Content

Sweat
Sour
From pain
Sweat
Sweet

From faith
In life

From
The awe
And wonder
Before us
Every day

Every
Privileged day

Your hands
Holding
Themselves
Palm
To palm
As

Your soul's
True path
Seeks
Eternity

Dignity
And love

Striving
Your hands
Have sought
For
God's

Creation
Everywhere

When
No other
Part
Of the
Soul
Remained
Willing
And
Few people
Few places
Expressed

Themselves

Capable

An octave
Of music
The
Touch

Of
A flower

Lily
Of the Valley
My most beloved
Flower
Rose up
As knowledge

Within
Your hands

Your hands
In
And of
Themselves
Unwilling
To fail
Your path

Unable

To fail
God

For me
They are
A signature
Your hands
No one

Has hands
Like them

They are
Yours
They
Somehow
Express
Every
Part
Of you

All
Of you

The
Holy
Embrace
Of
A man's
Life

I would
Know them

Anywhere
In eternity

With
Your hands
So precious
To me

Be
This
Absolute
Embrace
With
Every gesture

Embrace

Your
Children

The
Sacred
Trust
Of medicine
Your
True
Holy
And Perfect
Destiny

The
Very
Stars

The grace
That is
For you
And is
Ever

For
Your hands
In
Your hands
Your hands

I bless them

Precious hands
Precious man

RODEO

He had
affairs
at the
time
of the rodeo.

They entered
her bed
her soul
and
broke her heart.

He asked
wondered
with whom
shall
she stay
to pay me back.

The Wisteria
on
The Ile Saint Louis
perfect
above a wooden door

the Muguets des Bois,
Lilies of the Valley
with Grape Hyacinth
Leaves des Muguets
and Asparagus Fern.

Avec des nuages
with the clouds,
soft and grey
on days of heat
beauty
and soft rain.

I stayed with
them all

And with
you.

Paris, France

ENTRUST

He had
no affair
at the
time
of the rodeo.

No loss
entered
her bed
her soul
and
broke her heart.

He
asked
wondered
and
with
whom shall
she stay
in
Paris
to pay me back.

The
Wisteria
a
L'Ile Saint~Louis

perfect
above a wooden door

And
de
Muguet des Bois
Lily of the Valley
at
my
table
with Grape Hyacinth
Feuilles~Leaves~
des Muguet
and
Asparagus Fern.

Avec
des
nuages
With the clouds
soft and grey
on days of heat
beauty and soft rain.
I stayed with
them all.

And with
you.

Paris, France

YOUR WIFE

Wrinkles begin
At my lips
Of the old woman
Who is
Your wife
Constant
Faithful
Fruitful
True

HER HUSBAND

He is her husband
There is no other
Only him

Good
As
Soft
As
Cloud
Sweep
Over
The
Alps
Mist
Over
Bellagio
And
Strong
As
Granite
Schist
Faulted
Piercing
The
Autumn
In
Truth

WHITE

She was his wife.
No one
ever
thought
knew
him
with a wife
wed.

Her light was white
as the snow
black in the void
as a night
filled with the
stars of eternity
her
aspiration
for she wore the
hope of us
in us all.

That which
reaches eternity
and our pledge
to such.

NOBLE

Noble
As
Ancient
Great
Ones
And
Breathless
Words
Of
Courage
Certain
Words
Of
Stoics
Saints
Sages
Peasants
And
Kings
Guides
Of
History

Loving~
What
Would
Could
One
Say?
I love him.

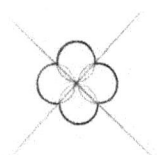

POEM FOR A STOIC

Turning
His head
That smile

Thunder

He became himself

One
With
His Father's
Voice
Voice of
His Father's Father
His Mother's Father

None
Saw
Him
Heard
Him
Felt
Him
Knew
Him

Only that
Which was
Thunder
Deeply awake
Like a goddess
A woman is quietly moved
To speak
To her stoic
In the very middle
Of the night
The words from God
Are specific
There are
Three

She is aware of them
Awake to them
And Heaven calls them
To her
Through her breath
And voice
To him
In the beautiful, beautiful
Dark

'I love you'

She caresses his arm
Her very life then
Speaks in one touch

To bless his
Which helps
All incarnations
Of all time
And space

The stoic moves
To the very edge
of their bed
His back against her,
He believes
He has heard
These words
Before

They cause him
Pain
She listens and
Many leaves rustle
In the Texas Spring
The most beautiful
Soft thunder calls
Rain patterns
The stone
Of their bedroom
Doorway
The varieties
Of birds call
The light
Of the time

Before dawn
Speaks
Carrying the sound
Of the sun's fire
To their Earth
To their hearth.

And she asks,
'We all love you,
Do you hear?'

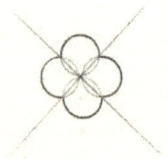

YOU WERE THERE

You were there
On the island
I waited for you
But
Yet
You were there
Already
And
All ready
Eternally.

You were there
On the island
I waited
For you.

For Joseph Brodsky
Venice, Italy

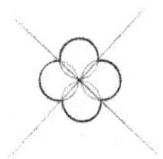

TRUE MARRIAGE

His
Wife

Not
One

Thought
Knew

Ever

There

Is

A wife

He
Loves

Her
Light

White

As
All

Snow

Black

In
The mind

As

A
Night

Filled

With

All
Stars

Their

Marriage

That

Hope

Of

All

That

Which

Reaches

Eternity

And our pledge
Marriage.

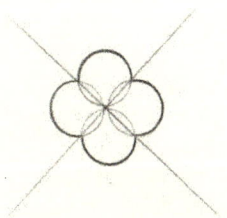

WHEN YOU KISS

When you kiss
someone
with your breath
you tell
the
truth
everything
you have
ever
been
everything
you may
ever be
is
in
your
breath
between
your
mouths
forever.
To
kiss
with
no
deceit

well
that,
beloved
is
to
know
God
Here.

YOU

You
Flow
Into me
I
Open
Like
A flower
Calling
The Ark
Of the Covenant
To
Open
Like
A key
As the lock
Turns
And the Christ
Comes again.

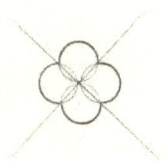

ABOUT THE AUTHOR

Elizabeth Anne Hin studied poetry formally with George E. Dimock, Richard Wilbur, William Hoover Van Voris, Michael Benedikt, Elizabeth Hardwick, Sir Stephen Spender, and Joseph Brodsky. Her Mother read poetry aloud from *A Child's Garden of Verses* by Robert Louis Stevenson and from other cherished texts from Beth's conception through childhood. Her Father taught her through his admiration for Homer's life, work, and virtuous message, from the world's classics and histories, and from noble and heroic peoples and cultures of all nations. He practiced his faith in the equality of all men and women, and in all aspiration: 'Ad astra per aspera,' ~Seneca. Her Mother was a private living example of this virtue.

Beth has embraced poetry, from reading to writing, since youth, observing in gratitude the poetry infused in sculpture at Wellington's port in New Zealand and attending readings by Jorge Luis Borges at the 92nd Street YMCA in Manhattan, New York, Adrienne Rich in a hallowed hall of Amherst, Massachusetts, Drummond Hadley and Gary Snyder in Anchorage, Alaska, Mary Oliver at a Presbyterian Church in Dallas, Texas. She has been shown kindness in mentoring by writers from John Updike to Carlos Fuentes, Richard Erdoes to Derek Walcott; and by W. S. Merwin, who expressed to her in 1973 that he had written nearly every day since the age of 21, and requested of Beth that she do the same.

ALSO BY ELIZABETH ANNE HIN

The Grail: A Story of Issa and Yeshua, 2014
Live Oak: Poems of Texas, 2016
Willow: Poems of Devotion, 2016.

Published by Issa Press; Austin, Texas

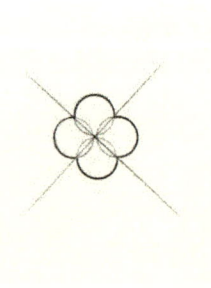

www.ingramcontent.com/pod-product-compliance
Lightning Source LLC
Chambersburg PA
CBHW022116090426
42743CB00008B/877